S0-ASG-777

NEW ZEALAND
LONG BRIGHT WORLD

BY THE SAME AUTHOR

Travel and Fiction

Tropical Quest (8th impression); Foyles Book Club choice; Adventurers Book Club choice
Eastern Quest (Foyles Book Club choice)
Wild Africa's Silent Call (Foreword by Peter Scott); Foyles Book Club choice
Let's Visit Kenya, Tanzania, Uganda (for the nine-to-eleven-year-old reader)
Safari with a Camera
Safari
The Motorist's Holiday Guide to Europe
The Photographer's Holiday Guide to Europe
A Guide to Germany (4th impression) American edition titled *Germany*
A Guide to Switzerland
Continental Autocamping
Townsend's Caribbean Guide (Foreword by His Excellency Donald C. Granado)
Townsend's Guide to East Africa and its National Parks
A Night in Trinidad (BBC Radio)
A Question of Psychology (BBC Radio)
Tag Along Tiger (BBC Radio)
The Long Road
The Green Drum
80,000 Mile Safari
Capricious Circles
Islands of the World (ABC Television)
Townsend's South Pacific Guide
7,100 islands—The Philippines (185 colour plates); designed by Stuart Harrison
The Air Travellers' Guide

Photographic

Underwater Photography (2nd impression, completely revised and reset)
Your A-Z Guide to Better Movies (also in paperback)
The Practical Guide to Holiday and Family Movies
How to use 16mm (also in paperback)
Filming in Colour (also in paperback)
Cine Photography (3rd impression)
Film in Research (5th impression)
Photographic Processing (2nd impression)
Guide to Movie Making
Sporting Photography
A Complete Guide to Home Movies
Glossary of Terms in Photography and Cinematography (four languages)
Glossary of Terms in Advertising and Public Relations (four languages)
Holiday Photography in Colour
Better Homes and Gardens—Photography for your Family (editor); American edition
Photography in Colour (BBC Radio and Television)
Industrial Photography
Advertising Photography

BY DEREK TOWNSEND AND TONY BARKER

Cannibals to Caviar (jacket and line illustrations by Stuart Harrison)
Ransom (jacket and line illustrations by Stuart Harrison)
Motoring Guide to Australia
Pacific Guide Volume 1
Pacific Guide Volume 2

NEW ZEALAND
LONG BRIGHT WORLD

DEREK TOWNSEND

THE
JACARANDA
PRESS

First published 1974 by
JACARANDA PRESS PTY LTD
65 Park Road, Milton, Q.
20 Falcon Street, Crows Nest, N.S.W.
37 Little Bourke Street, Melbourne, Vic.
142 Colin Street, West Perth, W.A.
303 Wright Street, Adelaide S.A.
57 France Street, Auckland, N.Z.
P.O. Box 3395, Port Moresby, P.N.G.
70A Greenleaf Road, Singapore 10
P.O. Box 239, Makati, Rizal, Philippines

Typesetting by
Queensland Type Service Pty Ltd, Brisbane

Printed in Hong Kong

National Library of Australia
Card Number and ISBN 0 7016 0730 0

Text and photographs by Derek Townsend
Design by Stuart Harrison and Barbara Hutley

Endpapers:
These depict one of Air New Zealand's magnificent wide-bodied, long-range DC-10 jetliners, whose lines exemplify the tranquillity and comfort of jet travel. On the tail, the distinctive, curved Koru motif symbolizes Air New Zealand's modern role in the Pacific. In another era, the design was carved on the stern posts of Maori canoes which probed the vast and unknown South Pacific.

The decorative motifs throughout this book are inspired by and based on the bulb-like Maori motif called Koru, which resembles the uncurling frond of a tree fern. This tendril-like motif is an essential element in Maori art.

Aotearoa, the Polynesian name for New Zealand, means Long White Cloud or Long Bright World.

Acknowledgments

The Author would like to thank Grant Easton of Mount Cook Airlines; Alex Gillett, W. F. Bern and E. R. Kelsey of the New Zealand Travel Commission in Wellington; W. Scott and S. O. J. Murphy of the New Zealand Travel Commission in Sydney; Craig Saxton of Air New Zealand who arranged special photography of Air New Zealand's DC10 in flight; The National Publicity Studios in Wellington who provided reference material of Maori art as well as specific photographs, which the author was not able to obtain, of skiing in New Zealand during winter; Fred ('Popeye') Lucas, his wife Lorie and son David; the personnel of NAC; Brenda Webb, Janice Thawe, Eleanor Morse, Julia Schuster, Beverley Vickers and Celia Turangi; the director and staff of the Maori Arts and Crafts Centre at Rotorua; the scores of everyday people in hotels, motels, buses, shops, bars and museums who all showed great friendliness and offered assistance wherever possible; for the beautiful little Maori girl Himah (page 58) who must surely grow up to become a 'model'; for those students who made the long bus journey from Te Anau to Dunedin pass so very quickly; for that wonderful lady in Dunedin who, although over sixty years old, is still an intrepid traveller/adventurer, artist and romantic; and last but not least to Stuart Harrison and Barbara Hutley who, together, are the most capable and enthusiastic design team I have yet found.

Author's Note

Many countries and their peoples have been depicted in books that are mainly composed of photographs. Yet, for me, even the best of these publications seem to lack complete communication; the pictures have no continuity and simply flash by, doing little to involve the reader/viewer.

In this book, by utilizing my experience of movie production and still photography, I have tried to capture the best of both worlds. Wherever possible, I have taken sequence pictures that 'open-up' a scene, each picture being an extension of the preceding shot. I have employed movie film techniques—first a long shot to establish the location, then a medium or medium close shot to show the main subject(s) in detail; then a close-up, or the occasional big close-up, to explore one special aspect or feature. Finally, the scene is further explored by shots taken from different angles and points-of-view.

Using this technique in a book, I have found the involvement to be much greater. Through such photographs, readers 'travel' around a particular country with an ever-increasing appreciation of its peoples and culture. To facilitate this process, the captions, generally, are more informative than usual and not repetitive information extracted from the text. Naturally, the photographs are of prime importance and thereby limit available writing space as well as somewhat curtail my usual style, once described as 'opinionated, unorthodox, occasionally sentimental, rather idiosyncratic but always fascinating'. Nevertheless, within these fourteen-thousand odd words of facts and figures, I have endeavoured to achieve some personalization while minimizing any detached 'neatness' that reports all the right things in a dirge of protective thoroughness.

I present here, no pseudo-encyclopedic precis, but an informative jaunt around New Zealand which I hope will also be entertaining.

CONTENTS

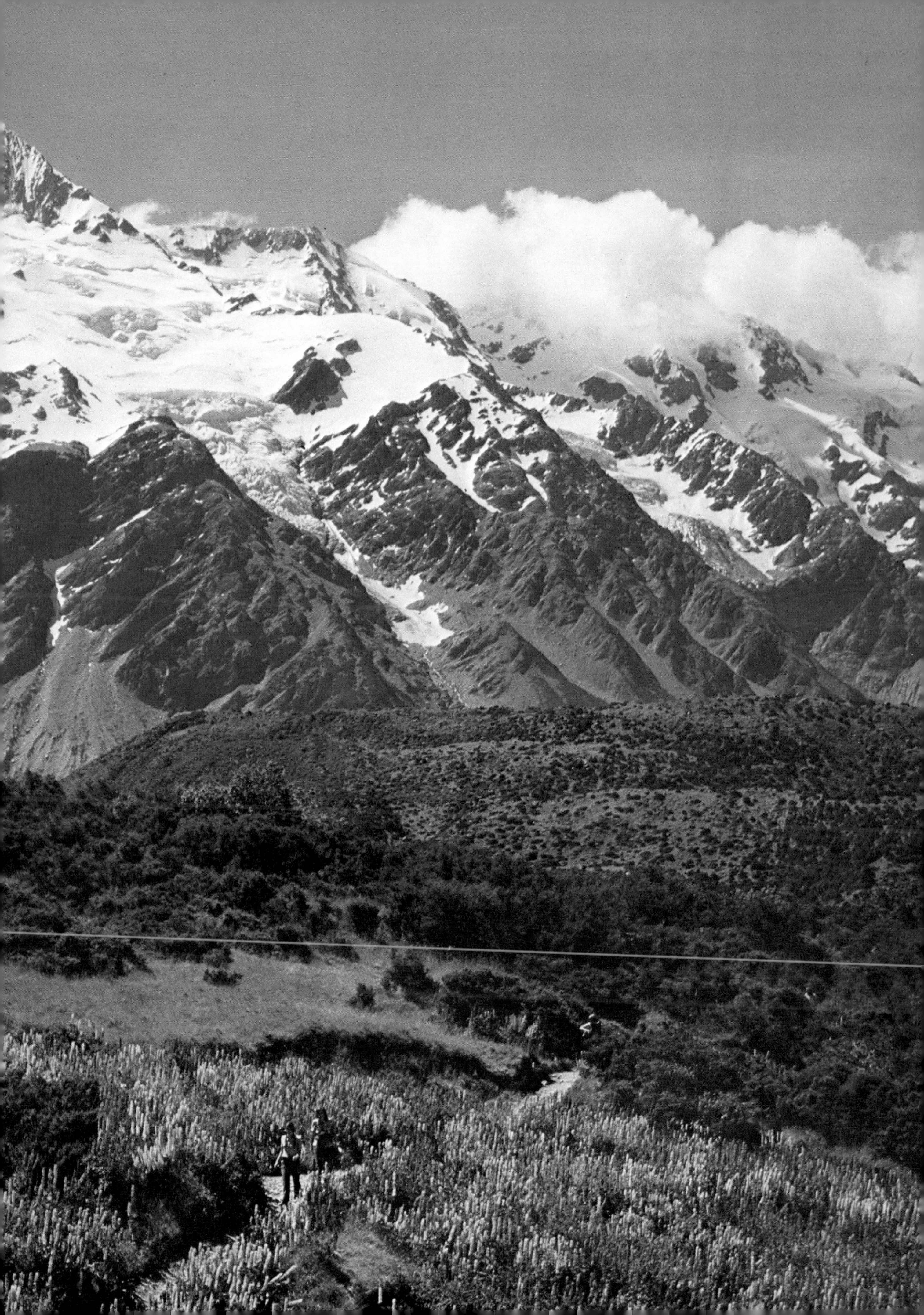

New Zealand is not a 'country' but a 'little world'. At every point of the compass, there is an infinite variety of scenery. One word—contrast—sums up the attractions. Though New Zealand is little bigger than Britain and situated outside the tropical Pacific, it is possible to experience a blizzard in the mountains or sunbathe on a burning, sandy beach. There are snow-formed glaciers that have carved huge fiords—and there are vast arid plains of colourful, subtropical vegetation. Between the two Islands there is also contrast: South Island is noted particularly for splendid alpine scenery and North Island for a unique area of thermal activity that incorporates everything from boiling lakes to mud geysers. Even the mountain passes differ in character. Some are bleak and remote; some are gentle and beautiful; others remain aloof and majestic.

Pages 8 and 9:
The Mount Cook National Park is at the centre of South Island; its perpetual snow-fields have few counterparts. These foothills form a base to the Alps which are often called 'Lords of the South'.

Page 10:
This small church in Queenstown could easily be in an English village.

Page 11:
In Rotorua especially, Maoris can be seen wearing their traditional dress. Descendants of intrepid fourteenth-century explorers from the mid-Pacific, the Maoris still keep alive their ancient heritage.

Pages 12 and 13:
The soft glow of summer dusk reflects on Lake Te Anau. A solitary float-plane merely emphasizes the isolation.

Page 14:
Napier City's Marine Parade is known locally as 'the golden mile'.

Page 15:
On the western side of this lake, notornis or takahe birds—thought to have been extinct for fifty years—were found in 1949.

Page 16:
Throughout New Zealand there are numberless Roman Catholic 'Homes of God', most of them built in unusual settings.

Introduction

> Today, there are few remaining accessible places where man can escape the imprisonment created by his own technological progress. Stone, metal, and cement fabrications devastate the world's surface. Industry pollutes the air we breathe. Highrise buildings keep the sunlight off our streets and blot out the stars. Indeed, these barriers so effectively isolate us from nature that many city children have never experienced even simple pleasures like smelling the early morning fragrance of flowers or the invigorating odour of damp earth.
>
> Yet, although the majority of people have had little opportunity to develop their perception and appreciation, they still retain an affinity with the essential qualities of life, for the womb of Mother Nature is where all humanity was nurtured.
>
> More than ever before, people need a retreat from their artificial environment, for the stimulus of the wilds awakens a new power of creation—it mellows—it soothes—it relaxes jangled nerves—it recharges the mental batteries. . . .

Five years ago (1969), I wrote these opening paragraphs as a Preface for my book *Wild Africa's Silent Call.* And in the same volume, Peter Scott wrote in *his* Foreword:

> I believe that something goes wrong with people when they cut themselves off from the natural world. This is why we keep gardens or window-boxes or house plants, or dogs or cats or budgerigars. Man does not live by bread alone, and never was this more true than today. I believe we should take just as great pains to look after the natural treasures which inspire us as we do to preserve the man-made treasures in art galleries and museums. This is a responsibility we have to future generations, just as we're responsible for the safeguarding of great works of art.
>
> It has been argued that if the human population of the world continues to increase at its present rate, there will soon be no room for either wild life or wild places, so why waste time, effort and money trying to conserve them now? But I believe that sooner or later we shall learn to limit out own over-population which, in my view, is one of humanity's greatest dangers. We shall become concerned with optimum rather than maximum, with quality rather than quantity, and everyone will rediscover the need for wild nature as an essential part of any high quality environment. . . .

Since *Wild Africa* was published, these quotations have become even more relevant. Over much of the world, rivers and lakes no longer support life in their murky filth. Forests are stripped and pastureland lies ruined. Construction engineers have blasted their way across the landscape with dynamite, scarring the countryside with roads, towns, factories and airports.

The once famous Italian Riviera coastlines of Liguria and Tirreno have become a nightmare of chemical plants, natural gas refineries and phosphate quarries. The Great Lakes of North America are open sewers—inanimate. Thousands of people have died from the effects of chemical smogs generated in great cities like Los Angeles, Tokyo and London. In the blue Pacific Ocean, hundreds of square kilometres are contaminated with radioactivity and classed as restricted danger zones.

From The Hermitage Hotel, visitors can make all types of excursions, from leisurely walks through mountain forest to strenuous climbs up rugged peaks. Few places in the world so vividly dramatize themselves as does this view (left) which lies immediately outside the hotel. During the summer months numerous species of mountain flowers—some rare—can be found along most tracks. (Text, page 47.)

Less than two kilometres away from The Hermitage, the mountains are already showing themselves more spectacularly. The triple peaks of Mount Cook itself, La Perouse, Mount Wakefield, The Footstool, Mount Ollivier, Mount Sefton and a dozen other grand peaks are all relatively close—the star attractions of an expanding tourist industry which lures visitors from lands far away.

Page 22: ▷
Apart from Maoris there are numbers of South Sea Islanders living throughout the country. This little girl was born in Rarotonga, one of the Cook Islands administered by New Zealand.

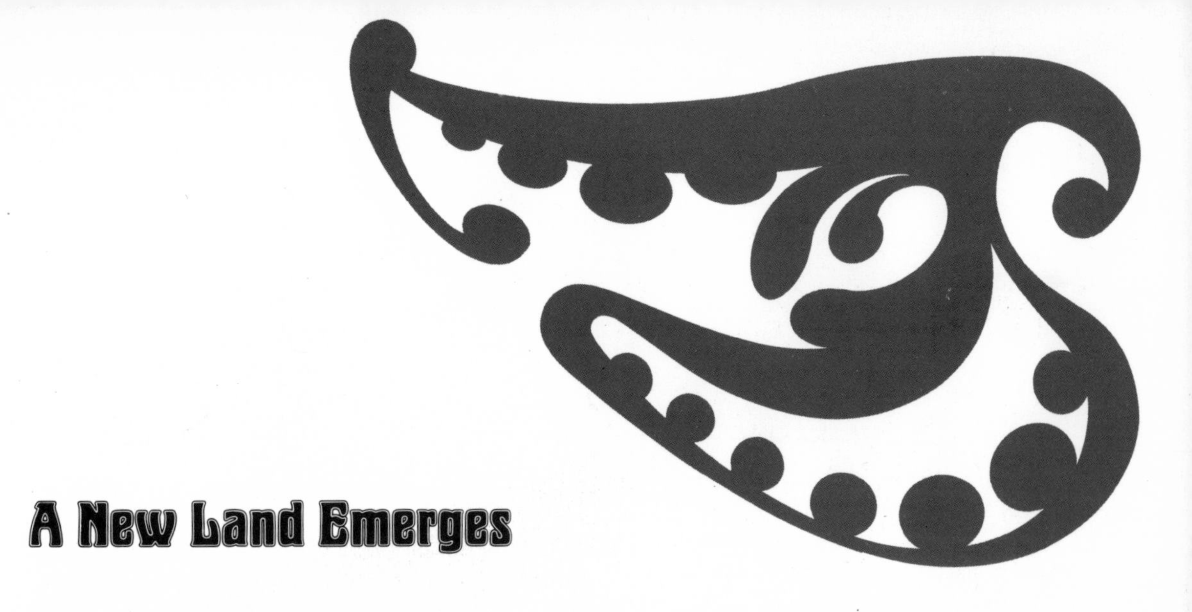

A New Land Emerges

With pollution spreading further and further around the globe, it is fortunate that much of the Pacific remains almost as remote as it appeared to early explorers. It is the biggest ocean—105 million square kilometres of water and larger than all the masses of our earth combined. It is also the deepest ocean—depths great enough to cover Mt Everest. And it is certainly the wildest ocean with volcanic upheavals and tidal waves.

Scattered across the Pacific are chains of tropical islands which, for generations, have lured adventurers. New Zealand is also a Pacific island. But it is not tropical. And unlike atolls with musical names such as Tahiti, Bora Bora, Moorea, Tikehau and Raiatea, there has been no extravaganza of praise from sentimentalists; no image of a time-defying magic and irresistible attraction. History and literature have not even endowed it with the mystique of being an earthly paradise.

Yet, New Zealand *is* an earthly paradise. Everything belonging to the great outdoors is brilliantly compacted in a mere fifteen-hundred-kilometre length; there are: snow-capped mountains with arrogant peaks; vast areas of rolling green pastures where the air is sweet; crystal lakes with water pure to drink; flowering glens; virgin forests mainly unexplored; remote fiords where the silent air is only disturbed by the crash of waterfalls that flash in the sunlight and tumble vertically from escarpments hundreds of metres above; bubbling geysers; and fertile valleys.

New Zealand suddenly rose out of the Pacific. It emerged as molten rock in a violent cataclysmic explosion with flaming balls of matter being hurled skywards for weeks on end. Eventually, this fiery upheaval settled, the boiling ocean became tepid, and the red-hot mass cooled to leave only a subterranean furnace. And there, beneath the prehistoric sun, was the miracle of New Zealand—a new land in the South Pacific. Centuries elapsed, and during this time glaciers of the ice-age carved deep valleys and fiords, scooped out lakes and shaped mountains. A few more hundred years passed. Numerous pieces of driftwood were caught on the jagged, razor-sharp, rocky coastline. Then sand, mud and sediment began to collect. Finally, migrant birds and the wind brought seeds across the pounding waves from land far away. By chance—or fate— these seeds fell into the sediment and soon green vegetation appeared. More earth accumulated. Frail trees grew

Left:
Queenstown Bay from the hillside behind the town overlooking Lake Wakatipu; across the water is Bob's Peak. In winter the surrounding mountains, with their jagged edges, are snow covered. Little more than a century ago, white explorers seeking new pastures looked upon this site for the first time. They were soon followed by gold-seekers who struck great wealth, particularly in the Kawaru River after the invention of gold dredges. (Text, pages 63 and 69.)
Below:
Typical Queenstown scenes. The modern church, both in design and setting, is reminiscent of Switzerland.

Left/below/page 27:
Queenstown's nearby peninsula is noted for its gardens where vivid flowers, lily ponds, exotic trees and shrubs overlook the town and beach. An enormous boulder has been inscribed as a memorial to the heroic polar explorer, Captain Robert Falcon Scott, R.N. In the same area there are also tennis courts, and bowling and croquet greens.

Left:
There are many launch trips available and the one to Mount Earnslaw is really worthwhile, especially on a calm day when the water reflects every surrounding peak. It is interesting to note that even today lake steamers are the only means of transport for many of the settlers who live in isolated sheep stations.
Below:
In the main shopping avenue, only pedestrians have access.

into sturdy forests. Sand fringed the inner shores. New Zealand was at last truly born and waiting for the advent of man.

THE COUNTRY

The two main islands of New Zealand are North Island, 820 kilometres long and up to 322 kilometres wide, and South Island, 772 kilometres by 335 kilometres; they are separated by the narrow Cook Strait. The total area is about one-sixth larger than that of Great Britain, and somewhat less than the State of California. New Zealand's position in the South Pacific is about half-way between the Equator and the South Pole; roughly the same in the southern hemisphere as that of Great Britain in the northern. From North America, the distance is 10 400 kilometres, and from Western Europe almost 20 000 kilometres; Australia lies 2240 kilometres to the north-west. The climate is temperate; North Island has been likened to Spain, and South Island to Austria.

The mountains of New Zealand can rival the Swiss Alps, the pastures are more luxuriant than England's, the waters have a more prolific fish life than those in Canada, the fiords could easily be Norwegian, and the beaches are generally far more appealing than Grand Anse, Playa de Aro, Waikiki, or a dozen other famed locations.

South Island is dominated by the impressive Southern Alps which rise to 3764 metres at Mount Cook and are snow-capped with many glaciers; seventeen peaks exceed 3000 metres. The south-west coast is cut into deep fiords. Of the glaciers, the Tasman (29 kilometres long) is the largest, but the Franz Josef and the Fox are equally well known, and have the unusual feature of descending to about 200 metres above sea-level where they actually reach into lowland vegetation. The numerous rivers are, in general, too short and rapid for navigation but are ideal for providing hydro-electric power. The Waikato, the Wanganui and Clutha are the most important, but all of them are under 483 kilometres long.

Although North Island has several mountain ranges, its peaks are less impressive; the active volcano Ruapehu (2795 metres) and the dormant Mount Egmont (2518 metres) are the tallest, with Ngauruhoe and Tongariro next. The rugged windward slopes of these mounts are rich with interesting vegetation, such as giant tree ferns which thrive in the warm moist air and help to evoke the atmosphere of New Zealand's evolutionary past. North of Ruapehu is Lake Taupo, sited in the centre of an incredible volcanic area which contains glaciers, boiling springs, hot mineral pools, solfataras, fumaroles, and bubbling mud lakes, many of them renowned for healing properties; this thermal region occupies a belt approximately 32 kilometres wide and 241 kilometres long.

Here then is a unique land where man can rediscover the need within himself for contact with wildness and wild nature as an essential part of life. This is New Zealand; a country where everything is fresh and blooming from the Creator. It is no wonder the Maoris called it *Aotearoa*, meaning 'long bright world' or 'long white cloud'.

.eft:
:ntrance to Cecil Peak Station. (Text, ›ages 69 and 73.)
ʔight/below:
The historic stone-built homestead is almost otally hidden from the camera by English ›ak, poplar, elder, ash, lime and ›ycamore trees.
\ place to relax; one of the twenty rooms vhich are full of antiques, oil paintings, ›olished mahogany furniture, brassware and :hina.
'he kea is a native bird that lives in high ocky crevices. It is friendly and inquisitive ›ut, says Mr Lucas, it attacks sheep, riding ›n their backs and probing with a sharp, ›ooked beak for the fat around the kidneys. ;heep attacked in this way die overnight rom blood-poisoning. (Many biologists do ›ot agree with these statements but to quote /Ir Lucas, *'I know* and I have seen. Those vho doubt only guess.')
'he last picture shows a guest bedroom.

.eft:
Iorses breed in the open at Cecil Peak and ıre acclimatized from birth to the colder vinters. The terrain contributes to the rowth of sound, strong-chested animals vith plenty of stamina. Pack-horses are still ecessary, either when mustering takes lace in the back-country or when fencing vork is to be done.
Right:
)uring each year, there are three main heep musters with the autumn one being he most important. A 'clean' muster is ssential because any sheep left behind arely survive the winter. Once the flocks ave been moved into their winter area, constant watch must be kept to prevent hem from climbing back above the nowline before the snow cap is established rmly. In the event of unexpected snow-torms, shepherds must begin 'snow aking'—searching for snowbound sheep nd battling through waist-deep snow to ring them safely to higher ground. In 1878, uring an exceptionally bad winter, Cecil eak lost more than 3000 sheep. emperatures were so low that the poor nimals were frozen to the ground while now on their backs, sometimes 200 milli-etres thick, was frozen in solid lumps. nother bad time was 1968 but losses were educed considerably by the New Zealand ir Force who flew from dawn to dusk rrying hay and men to the twenty stations eeding help.

From the waters of Milford Sound rise the sheer walls of Mitre Peak, known as the 'Monarch of Milford'. North of this point the fiords are deep enough to take ocean liners and aircraft carriers. Milford Sound is the most dramatic inlet of Fiordland National Park. Maoris from the west coast of Otago Province used to visit the sound until Europeans arrived seeking the precious 'tear-drop' gemstone called tangiwai. The Maori name for Milford Sound is *Piopiotahi.* Reference material about the official name is confusing. It seems undecided whether the Sound was named in 1829 by Captain John Grono or a year later by Captain John Stokes, R.N. However, it was definitely named after Milford Haven in Wales. And in 1821, Captain Stokes did visit the Sound and described it in his log as 'the most remarkable harbour yet visited by the *Acheron* in New Zealand'.

NATURAL FLORA AND FAUNA

New Zealand is of particular biological interest because three-quarters of its flowering vegetation is endemic, and the majority bear no resemblance to those of Australia or even to nearby Polynesian islands. In North Island are kauri pines, giants of the old forest world; in South Island are pure stands of one or other of the five New Zealand species of *Nothofagus* (beech). Lakesides are brightened by trees such as the kowhai (*Sophora microphylla*) with its yellow blooms. Beautiful flowers include the giant scarlet rata (*Ranunculaceoa* family; mountain lily) and the attractive pohutukawa (*Metrosideros excelsa*), often called New Zealand Christmas Tree.

The endemic fauna is likewise peculiar due to the long geological isolation of the country which, from available facts, must have occurred before the evolution of mammals. There are no marsupials or snakes—even the dogs and rats are imported, though by accident.

Because there were no predatory animals, many birds—such as the quaint kiwi and rare takahe—have lost their power of flight. (The takahe bird was thought to be extinct, but in 1948 they were rediscovered in a remote valley where they are now protected in 200 000 hectares of natural habitat which has been declared a 'closed sanctuary'.) Unfortunately, wingless cranes are extinct and so are the various kinds of moa which stood up to four metres high and had hairless feathers like the kiwi. Other native birds include the kaka (*Nestormeridionalis*), a green and brown forest parrot; the morepork owl (*Ninox novaeseelandiae*), the rare white heron (*Egretta alba*) and the fantail (*Phipidura fuliginosa*).

But the most famed zoological peculiarity is the tuatara, a lizard-like creature which is a 'living fossil', and is the only surviving member of the *Rhynchocephalia*, an order of reptiles dating from the end of the Primary era, long before the dinosaur appeared. The tuatara is more than half a metre long and is green in colour with a vestigial third eye on the top of its skull; its existence shows that in those 'early' days, New Zealand must have then had a connexion with the world's bigger land masses. The tuatara's life span is thought to be more than a hundred years.

THE COMING OF MAN

New Zealand was first inhabited by the Maoris—a Polynesian people thought to be of South Asian origin—who migrated from the Asiatic mainland. The Polynesians are natural sailors; they regard pitting their wits against the sea as no more than an enjoyable challenge, and their explorations in frail craft throughout the vast and stormy Pacific show a courage, initiative, skill, strength and seamanship that have never been equalled. When one speaks of Cook, Magellan, Bougainville, Fernandez de Quiros and Drake, although not belittling their achievements, it is rarely appreciated that the real discoverers of the Pacific were the Polynesians who had none of the resources available to great European pioneers. Navigating by instinct and a self-taught knowledge of the stars, and using primitive boats, the Polynesians

On the road from Te Anau to Milford Sound are the 'Mirror Lakes', surrounded entirely by forest and reflecting the mountains so clearly that, on gazing into the water, it is possible to become disorientated. 'Am I standing on my head or on my feet?'

Page 38:
This journey to Milford Sound is one of the most beautiful and varied in South Island. The picture, bottom right, shows part of the avalanche area close to Homer Tunnel. (Text, page 77.)
Page 39:
There are many points of interest to see from a vessel on the Sound: Bowen Falls, the glacier of Mount Pembroke, Harrison Cove, Lion Rock and Stirling Falls are but a few of them.

Above:
Near to Milford there are many desolate beaches and wild rivers.
Page 42: ▷
Launch trips are the best way for visitors to explore the Milford fiord. The launches chug along the steep, wooded slopes whose lower portions, in season, are vivid with scarlet mistletoe and other colourful flowering shrubs. When nearing the mighty waterfalls, a launch is dwarfed into insignificance.

TUTOKO
TUTOKO

spread out in all directions. Basing themselves in Tahiti, Samoa and Tonga, they travelled south almost to the Antarctic, and north as far as the Hawaiian islands. While Europeans still believed the world to be flat and were afraid to venture even into the Atlantic, these amazing brown-skinned people had completed all the major Pacific explorations.

If I appear to be labouring this point of Polynesian conquest, it is only because few credits have been given. Additionally, Europeans who may glance at an atlas can rarely comprehend the vastness of such an ocean when it is represented only by a small blue section on the map. With great tidal waves and the worst ocean storms in the world, the 'Pacific' belies its name.

Traditionally, the discovery of New Zealand is accredited to Kupe who, around the middle of the tenth century A.D., was said to have sailed his canoe either from Rarotonga in the Cook Islands or from Raiatea in the Society Group. Others followed. Then came Toi, a Maori navigator from Tahiti, who led more settlers to the new land. They populated the two main islands and named their tribes after the canoes in which they had made the long journey—Arawa, Ngapuhi, Wharetoa, to name but three. Here, with an abundance of fish, birds, roots and berries, food was never short and life was good. They hunted the giant moa, trapped smaller birds in the air and on the ground, caught eels, farmed the land, and loved and died.

Abel Janszoon Tasman, a Dutch navigator, was the first European to sight New Zealand, in the year 1642; but after losing four of his men in a skirmish with the Maoris, Tasman sailed away without setting foot on the land. Apart from making a few crude maps, he apparently deemed his discovery unimportant and made no attempt to return. However, his pilot, the hydrographer Visscher, wrote a *Memoir Concerning the Discovery of the Southland*, in which he recorded, on 13 December 1642, that Tasman sighted 'a great land uplifted high'; so perhaps New Zealand did at least make an impression upon one of these first European discoverers.

It was 127 years later when Europeans once again reached New Zealand. This time it was the British seafarer, Captain James Cook, who arrived from Tahiti in the *Endeavour* and made his landing on 7 October 1769 at Poverty Bay on North Island. Cook immediately claimed the land for the British Crown; and, in 1840, after years of bloody fights with the proud Maori settlers, the Treaty of Waitangi was eventually signed. Under this treaty, the Maori people accepted British sovereignty in exchange for citizenship and guarantees of land and food resources.

Today, a journey through New Zealand allows people to see a new Pacific country in the making; for just as the Polynesians left their warm islands to make new homes in *Aotearoa*, so white settlers have sailed from Great Britain to carve their destiny in the new land far south of Asia. Some 2.75 million people live peaceably in New Zealand; 180 000 of these are of the Maori race who enjoy full civic rights. (The name Maori derives from the term *tangata maori*, meaning 'man native to the place'.) And over the plains, which were once the habitat of giant moa, roam 60 million sheep and 8 million head of cattle.

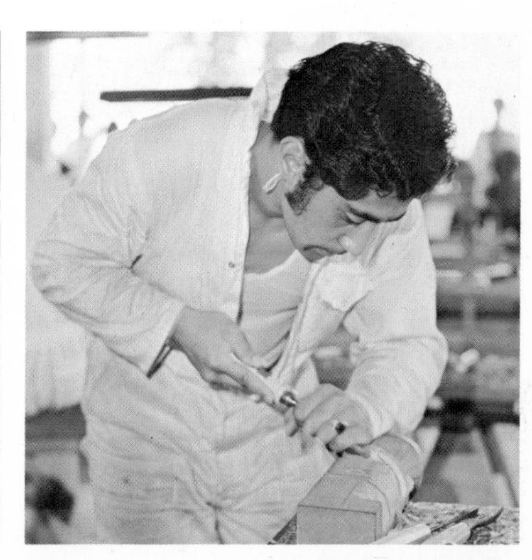

eft:
he tiki, visible in this picture, belongs ssentially to the Maori people of New ealand. Originally, the tiki was an rnament which resembled a grotesque uman figure and was worn by women as a ertility emblem. The most treasured tikis ere made of gemstone, a dark translucent ephrite found mainly in the west of South sland. Over the centuries, the original form nd meaning of the tiki have both been ost'; it has now become New Zealand's ood luck symbol.

age 45:
otorua is the centre of Maori culture. ancing, carving and weaving are all aditional skills kept alive today. (Text, age 115.)

My own arrival in New Zealand was far removed from the early Polynesian days; instead of arriving by giant ocean-going canoe, I landed on South Island at Christchurch airport in the latest giant of the skies—an Air New Zealand DC10 with a length of seventy-one metres and a tail, vividly distinguished by a Maori motif, soaring to twenty metres above the ground. We had navigated by radio signals, not by the stars. And our journey had taken hours instead of months.

However, my immediate destination was not Christchurch—New Zealand's second largest city—but Mount Cook, and already I had transferred to an NAC jet prop Avro bound for the remote airstrip located 762 metres above sea-level and surrounded by the highest peaks in the Alps.

Because of fine weather our captain elected to make a low-level scenic approach through the mountainous terrain. He partly lowered the aeroplane's flaps, to reduce stalling speed, and thereby enabled us to fly more slowly while negotiating the contours of a narrow, curving valley where our wing tips seemed almost about to scratch the snowy walls.

With propeller revolutions reduced to a minimum, the hypnotic engine drone induced a strange tranquillity. We were suspended in an aestheticism of unreality, having no connexion either with the white ruggedness below or with the blue-violet of space above. There were constant 'oohs' and 'ahs' from the passengers; the whir of movie cameras; the chatter of voices—Japanese, Chinese, English, Indian and other nationalities, all mingling with audible expression of visual pleasure.

The Hermitage Hotel stands at the centre of Mount Cook National Park, an area comprising snowfields, glaciers, alpine grasslands and herb fields, forests, lakes, waterfalls and rivers. From the hotel lounge there is a perfect view of *Aorangi* (Cloud Piercer), the name given by Maori tribesmen to Mount Cook, the country's highest elevation. True, it does not have the fascinating mystique of Everest or Kilimanjaro, nevertheless Mount Cook (3764 metres) is mighty enough to exhibit an inspiring beauty. And like kittens with their mother, a myriad smaller mountains cluster around and spread from the majestic peak in all directions. A kilometre or so from The Hermitage they become merely foothills on which masses of blue, pink, white and purple lupins stand proud and erect, leaving the air heavy with perfume.

Sub-alpine scrub supports more than 300 species of native plants, which, scattered amid the lower green slopes, produce eye-catching areas of colour that vary from a yellow, brighter than buttercups, to an incandescent red. Here is a wild garden virtually untrampled by man and set against the grandeur of highland country where 140 snowy tips exceed more than 2 kilometres. Surely this is how everything must have been 'in the very beginning'.

Generally, early mornings are clear and windless. This is the best time for taking a ski-plane trip in a six-seater Cessna to the Tasman Glacier. The

Left:
Dunedin, the port and Capital of Otago, was well served by Charles Kettle. He laid out the original town and, at the same time, planned for a much larger city, although he could not have guessed at today's expansion over the hills and valleys. But the very early settlers were given wise counsel, 'Make the country accessible; enable people to go and settle and flourish in the country, instead of desponding and idling in the town. Never fear for your town as long as your country prospers; never hope for it as long as the country is a desert.' And to New Zealand society the people of Dunedin have made a splendid contribution in 'programmes' that cover everything from dental care and education to unemployment and local architecture. (Text, pages 95 and 99.)
Right/top:
St Paul's Cathedral dominates the Octagon. Instead of the traditional square, Dunedin is built around an Octagon with trees and flowerbeds as well as a statue of the Scottish poet, Robert Burns, in the centre.
Right/bottom:
'The Home', in Dunedin's Glenfalloch Woodlands Gardens, is reached via an interesting waterside drive along the shore of Otago Harbour.

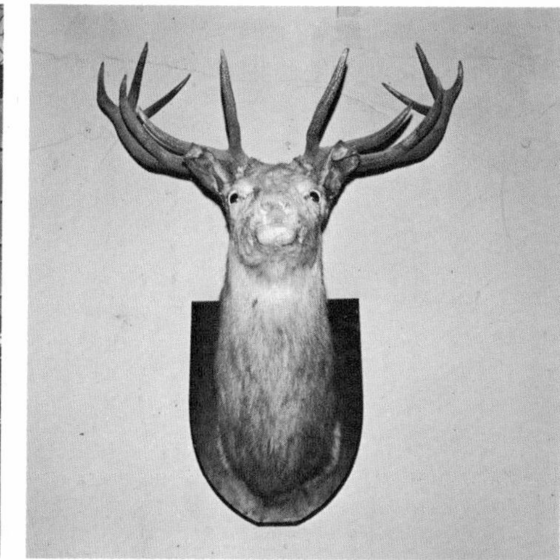

eft:
anarch Castle, built in Dunedin with
aterials bought all over the world—marble
om Italy, glass from Venice, tiles from
ngland, wood from Canada. These were
nported at a time when sailing ships took
onths to make the journey. Then,
verything had to be brought across the
ver on a punt and finally dragged up the
eep hill by ox-drawn wagons. (Text,
age 99.)
ight:
few of the rooms to be seen in this castle.
he marble fireplace is genuine Italian;
e piano is much older than the building
self; the lion head is associated with
e Lanarch family crest motto of *Sans Peur*
Vithout Fear).

Chaotic patterns in snow and ice—the
Southern Alps.

flights are undertaken by Mount Cook Airlines, a company which has been operating both scheduled and charter scenic services for more than fifty years. The outbreak of World War II forced the airline to sell all its aeroplanes, and flying did not recommence at Mount Cook until 1952; even then it was confined to joy-rides, crop-dusting, supply-dropping and the inevitable rescue mission. During these trips, pioneer Harry Wigley would often fly over the tremendous snowfields at the heads of the Tasman, Fox and Franz Josef Glaciers and wonder how they could be exploited. As a mountaineer he knew the excitement of standing on these vast, lofty snowfields; and if the problem of inaccessibility could be solved, there was no doubt they would become a great tourist attraction. Wigley approached the problem by combining two of his favourite activities—skiing and flying.

The obvious answer was retractable skis which could be raised to allow the aircraft to take off on its wheels from a grass airfield and then lowered to land on the snowfields at the heads of the glaciers. These were manufactured in the Mount Cook Company's garage at Timaru.

In September 1955, Harry Wigley with Alan 'Squib' McWhirter, who is today Mount Cook Airlines' traffic manager at Christchurch, took off from The Hermitage in the first ski-equipped aircraft. At first a low-level run was made over a smooth area of snow on the upper Tasman Glacier to enable 'Squib' to throw out pieces of foliage every five or so seconds to mark out a runway. The skis brushed the snow very gently and they settled down with no vibration, noise or bouncing; so smooth and effortless, it was almost an anticlimax. During the day several more trips to the snowfields were made with a number of passengers; and in 1956, after meeting all commercial safety requirements, regular flights from The Hermitage to the glaciers commenced. In 1972, 33 000 passengers were carried on alpine flights; passengers on the ski-planes are of different ages and nationalities, and have included heads of state, film stars and a wide cross-section of celebrities.

The ski-planes have also enabled the skiing potential of the Tasman Glacier to be fully exploited. They are used more and more by skiers, who take off from the Hermitage airfield with their skis strapped to the wing of the aeroplane and are landed at the Saddle, close to 2.5 kilometres above sea-level. From here they can enjoy a downhill run of about 8 kilometres to Darwin Corner. At this point skiers can choose to return to the Saddle by ski-plane for a repeat run or to carry on for about 13 kilometres down the glacier to the Ball Hut, returning by road to The Hermitage.

The Tasman has a main ski season from June to October inclusive but, with favourable winter conditions, it is possible to ski the whole year round. Parties are provided with a guide and, due to the nature of the 'run', skiers will be accepted only after proving to be of a competent standard. The minimum party is three skiers and up to twenty-three can ski the run.

However, even visitors, who cannot recognize the difference between a pair of skis and two surfboards, should take the ski-plane trip; to use a travel brochure cliche, 'It is a must'.

Left:
Wellington, the capital, is surrounded by the hills of Port Nicholson. The harbour occupies a basin formed by a buckling of the earth's crust. During the great earthquake of 1855, Wellington's Marine Drive beach rose almost two metres. From the air, older raised shorelines can be seen bordering Cook Strait at Cape Palliser, Baring Head and Tongue Point. Volcanic faults account for many of the nearby islands and peninsulas. (Text, pages 89 and 95.)

Below:
The botanical gardens, the marble-faced House of Parliament and the harbour are just a few of the attractions in Wellington. (There are conducted tours of the parliament building.)

Below/Right:
Lady Norwood Rose Gardens are set in parklike surroundings and are within easy reach of the capital either by trolleybus or by cable car. The Norwood Begonia House has an all-year-round display of plants.
Page 58: ▷
For this little girl trying to cool-off, the gardener has turned 'a blind eye'. Even the goldfish seem not to resent the intrusion!

The author is a qualified and capable pilot; nevertheless, this landing on the Tasman was an unrivalled scenic memory. I have had no opportunity to develop that special skill and judgment necessary for mountain flying; over mountains, yes, but never anything to compare with this experience. Zooming down into snow-locked valleys; then up, banking, scraping over precipitous ledges of ice.

And nearing the glacier we flew straight towards mighty cliff walls which rose perpendicularly to dizzy heights above us. Our speed remained steady at 140 knots. Our course never varied. Now the walls overwhelmed us with their apparent closeness and still we held that speed and course. Every instinct told me to make a steep turn before it was too late. Yet my fellow passengers showed no apprehension; their awe was for the peaks our pilot was pointing out in detail. Distance was certainly deceptive. Those cliffs were obviously still a long way off. But, at last, the turn was made; gently and without hurry. Almost simultaneously, revolutions were reduced to a mere 1800. Flaps 20 degrees. Already the airspeed had fallen to 100 knots. We were preparing to land. Airspeed 85 knots. Flaps 30. The descent steepened. We had to land at once. But where? I could see only an impossible steep area of virgin snow. The stall warning howled and we touched down smoothly on an enormous glacier. It was flat. Mile upon mile of perfect runway without an obstruction; my impression of steepness had come from what is know as 'mountain disorientation'.

The sky was azure. And the sun burned my face and the snow numbed my feet as I crunched noisily across this solitude of ice. Climbing and slithering to a high vantage point, I watched an isolated storm sweeping across the western landscape. Rainbow tentacles, falling from the black sky like carnival streamers, were reflected from ice walls in a kaleidoscope of colour. Nearer, variegated cloud formations snaked across the panorama immediately below, stamping a final touch of splendour on this great wilderness where our Cessna aeroplane had suddenly assumed the insignificance of a discarded toy; and even my very existence had become a microcosm.

Some places of interest to visit from The Hermitage:

Hochstetter Ice Fall: A solid mass of tumbling ice almost 1.25 kilometres high. It is fed by the Linda Glacier and the Grand Plateau. A fascinating glacier to explore.

Hooker Hut: At an altitude of a kilometre or so, this hut is the departure point for both the Copland and Ball Passes.

Red Lakes: Approximately an hour and a half from The Hermitage. Outstanding views of Mt Cook and other major peaks. For the energetic, a further climb, to the top of Mt Sebastopol, takes about an hour. The views are even more rewarding.

Malte Brun Hut: Sixteen kilometres up the Tasman Glacier from Ball Hut. In this area, the beauty of the mountains is legendary.

Left/Right/Below:
In and around the capital; spring, summer, winter. The Marine Drive, beginning at Oriental Parade, is one of the world's longest. Many fine beaches and lakes are accessible. Lyall Bay is excellent for surfing.

Mt Wakefield: The last peak on the Mt Cook range. The summit gives spectacular views of all parts of the Mt Cook National Park. A climb requiring extra energy, but without any technical difficulties. The descent, by way of the scree or shingle slide opposite Glencoe Lodge, is direct and easy.

Sealy Lakes: The imposing face of Mt Sefton is best seen from the area around Mueller Hut about three hours from The Hermitage.
Sealy Lake, a small mountain tarn, lies halfway up to the Hut from the Kea Point track. The lake is quite suitable for swimming.

Copland Pass: One of the most interesting and exciting trips available in the Mt Cook area. (It is not necessary to have had previous mountaineering experience when crossing with a guide.) Crampons and ice-axe are necessary for the crossing but can be hired. The views from the crest of the Main Divide are as spectacular as any others in New Zealand, and the Copland Valley is one of the most impressive and beautiful in the Westland National Park. Tracks, huts and bridges are well maintained and in good condition. Not all creeks are bridged.

Graham Saddle: This trans-alpine crossing is an interesting journey of two to three days and provides an opportunity to learn something more of basic snow and icecraft techniques. An extremely rewarding and enjoyable trip for people of above average fitness. Prior climbing experience not essential when accompanied by a guide. Nights are spent at de la Beche and Almer Huts. The journey includes an ascent or descent of the Tasman, Rudolf and Franz Josef Glaciers.

Tasman Glacier: By coach. After leaving The Hermitage, a turn north into the Tasman Valley beyond the Hooker Bridge provides first views of the moraine-covered terminal of the Tasman Glacier, dominated by the lofty peaks of the Malte Brun range beyond. Further up the valley, Mt de la Beche and the Minarets can be seen. Other features en route include the source of the Blue Stream, gushing in springs from a large shingle fan; parts of the old horse-track formed late last century; and finally a superb view of the great, hummocky, rock-covered, lower reaches of the Tasman. As the road leaves the narrow crest of moraine, the snowy summit of Mt Cook comes into view high above on the left. Reasonably fit people can negotiate the access track to the glacier itself, and then cross the moraine and ice, for a round-tour of two kilometres.

HAVEN FOR A QUEEN

The journey from Mount Cook to Queenstown airport, in Central Otago, takes forty minutes. This resort was so named because, in 1863, the site was said to be 'fit for a Queen'. As this meant the punctilious and exacting Queen Victoria, I feel there is little need to emphasize the perfection of Queenstown's setting on beautiful Lake Wakatipu.

It *has* been written, 'you would have to go to Kashmir or Switzerland or

Nightclubs are rare and usually disappointing, although this one in Wellington did offer some expertise and colour in the dance-strip routines. (Text, page 89.)

Left/below:
Visitors can bathe in the hot, mineral waters at *Polynesian Pools* in Rotorua. Outside, there are sunbathing decks in garden surrounds overlooking Lake Rotorua and Sulphur Point. (Text, page 115.)
Page 68:▷
Emerald Pool, Waimangu Thermal Valley, Rotorua. (Text, page 109.)

Northern Italy to find a place like Queenstown'. I do not agree. None of these 'places' offers anything to compare with Queenstown. Kashmir can produce sunless, unpleasant periods of ice-cold weather, and has long been 'run down' as a resort. Switzerland has tremendous appeal, but all Europe is over-populated and the boom of tourism to this small country means crowded places almost everywhere. And for years, Italy has been off the tourist map as far as *my* recommendations are concerned; industrial pollution has taken too great a toll.

But Queenstown, with its true 'four-season' climate and fine scenery, is set among the world's best lake and mountain resorts. Comparatively, tourism here is only just beginning and the visitor can enjoy a wide variety of activities without the discomfort of always having to queue for over-crowded facilities: you can take a journey through a wild gorge to the rich gold strike area of Maori Point; see the great forests of Paradise Fall; ride by fast gondola to a restaurant at Bob's Peak, 438 metres above the town; whisk up Coronation Peak (more than 1.5 kilometres high) in a chairlift; or for something even faster, get a near panic thrill by taking a 30-knot jet boat up the Shotover Rapids. (A large power unit sucks up and ejects water through high-pressure stern nozzles that raise the boat to about 75 millimetres above the rapids and enable it to travel just as fast in either direction, irrespective of current speed.)

A SHEEP STATION AT WORK

Possibly, the most rewarding of the side attractions from Queenstown is a visit to Cecil Peak, a fully-operational, high-country, sheep station covering 137 kilometres. Its owner-boss is Fred Lucas, an ace bomber pilot in World War II (he won two Distinguished Flying Crosses), who carried his flying expertise into private life and pioneered a successful aviation business before he sold out and bought the remote Cecil Peak.

Over the last ten years or so, Fred—or 'Popeye' as he is known from North to South Island—has lived on this station with his wife and four sons. (His nickname derived from the way he rolled his false teeth and puckered his face.) They have now played host to a quarter-of-a-million visitors, and last year alone twenty-five thousand came from the United States.

Cecil Peak can only be reached by boat or helicopter and, with practically all the boundaries being water, it is virtually an island. The station lies across Lake Wakatipu from Queenstown and I boarded the *Viking*, a high-speed, sixty-six passenger, cruise launch 'skippered' by David Lucas, the second oldest Lucas son. While making the twenty-minute crossing, he recounted a legend dating back to the first Maoris who settled around the lake; apparently, they believed this stretch of water contained the soul of Matau, an evil giant. Certainly the lake has a peculiarity for which science has so far given no final explanation; every fifteen minutes there is a regular seventy-six-millimetre rise and fall of its waters. Maoris explained this phenomenon by saying it was Matau's soul breathing and it was the mood of his soul which controlled whether the water was rough or smooth.

Pages 70-72: ▷
Scenes around Rotorua and Waimangu Valley. (Text, pages 109 to 115.) Maori carvings are produced by experts, and examples of their 'work' in very early days can be seen everywhere. A picturesque church in the nearby village of Ohinemutu is noted for excellent decorations in wood. There also is an attractive meeting house where Maoris can always be seen. (*Below:* Even the public 'loo' is embellished with carvings!) At the entrance to Whakarewarewa Maori village, throw a coin into the water and children will retrieve it by making the necessary high dive from the bridge or from the rocks.

Disregarding any legend, Wakatipu is impressive. Shaped like an elongated 'S', it stretches for 84 kilometres; one spot has been plumbed to almost 396 metres and the water is said to be 98 per cent pure; the locals use it in their car batteries!

Mr Lucas was waiting at the jetty when we arrived and everyone piled quickly into a battered, old Daimler bus. 'Don't break any of the spiders' webs; I'm breeding them,' he said. 'Now, everybody hold tight because, if the engine ever starts and we don't fall apart in the first minute, we should be doing five miles an hour up the hill. . . . If you smell anything strange it's either the bus on fire or me; I've just come from the woolshed. You know, it's really quite funny; for years I've been fleecing sheep and now I'm fleecing the tourists as well. In fact, I might just stick with the tourists; they're usually easier to handle. Mind you, there's a few I would have liked to handle, but the dogs have been taught to get me if I even look that way inclined.' He turned around and scrutinized us briefly, 'You lot needn't worry. Just look at those hillsides, even the dogs get vertigo.' And so the patter continued.

All too quickly the kilometre trip ended at the century-old homestead, where Lorie Lucas welcomed us with tea (served from antique silverware) and masses of homebaked scones and cakes. Then Fred took us all for an informative and entertaining guided tour.

The station has always run merino sheep and recent flock numbers reached 8500. They are bred only for wool, and surplus sheep are sold or used to provide the station with meat for the table. Those past their prime are used to feed the working dogs. During the main muster there are often 60 dogs and this means killing 6 sheep every night. Lambing percentages are nowhere as high as on lowland farms and it is difficult to breed replacements let alone create a surplus. A depressed wool industry has meant a temporary reduction in flocks to less than 1000 sheep, but even with reduced numbers the routine of sheep work remains the same. Activities such as eye-clipping, crutching and foot-rotting continue.

With eye-clipping, the wool is shorn from over the eyes so the animal can see to graze and feed. If this is not undertaken, sheep become wool-blind and often starve or even fall over cliffs. In crutching, wool is removed from the hind-quarters to leave the animal clean and resistant to flies and germs. Foot-rotting is the use of an antiseptic to kill an organism that infects the foot beneath the hoof, causing extreme pain and lameness.

With the drop in wool prices, plans to begin cattle rearing were accelerated. By 1969 Cecil Peak had more than 450 Hereford breeding cows. Two years later 700 young, in-calf heifers and 21 stud Hereford bulls were bought from a neighbouring station. With the heifers already acclimatized, they produced a 70 per cent success in calving, thereby making the operation viable.

Yet another venture is horse breeding. But then, Cecil Peak is great horse country with lime outcrops and plenty of good grass. For houseguests, horses and ponies are always available.

Anybody can stay at Cecil Peak; and it provides one of the most unusual, stimulating, and peaceful vacations possible.

HOT WATER CREEK
FLOW RATE 1200 GALS PER MIN.
TEMP. 120/150° FAH 47/65° CENT

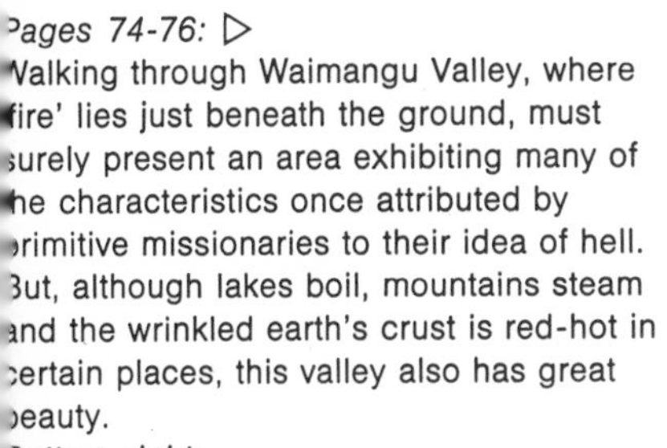

Pages 74-76: ▷
Walking through Waimangu Valley, where 'fire' lies just beneath the ground, must surely present an area exhibiting many of the characteristics once attributed by primitive missionaries to their idea of hell. But, although lakes boil, mountains steam and the wrinkled earth's crust is red-hot in certain places, this valley also has great beauty.
Bottom right:
Orange, brown, black, white and green all intermingle and to the layman may appear as stagnation, but in fact are caused by algae and numerous mineral deposits. Delicate silica flowers grow on the surrounding banks. Where the water is a rusty-brown, iodine is present in fairly large concentrations.

The Waimangu track ends on the shores of Lake Rotomahana. Beneath the blue water lie the famous Pink and White Terraces which were destroyed in 1886 when Tarawera erupted. Cliffs surrounding the lake continually steam.

The Province of Otago, with an area of 38 850 square kilometres, is about the same size as Switzerland, the Netherlands, Taiwan or Denmark. The essential difference is that, while the population of Otago is only a fraction of these four countries, it still enjoys many of the same diverse features, especially with regard to landscape. Central Otago is typified by Queenstown. But the eastern Pacific coast has hundreds of kilometres of beaches, some rugged, others with white sand. And the west coast, from Haast in the north to Milford Sound in the south, is one of the world's largest national parks; it covers 1·2 million hectares and is known as Fiordland. An area where, in 1773, Captain Cook spent five weeks in wild and uninhabited glacier retreats, surrounded on all sides by water—in the west by the cold sea and in the east by melted snows dammed naturally behind morainic debris.

(Although Central Otago is merely 64 kilometres from the west coast, there is a startling contrast between the well-watered, sunny west [six metres of rain with 2000 sunshine hours] and the desert-like central area that receives only a 330-millimetre rainfall. Rich, lush-green plains and sub-tropical rainforest quickly merge into arid, sunlit hills of colourful vegetation which were settled by the Scots in 1859; European trees, planted by early gold-seekers, brighten every lakeside and river bank.)

Of all the 'spectaculars' in Fiordland, Milford Sound is probably the most famous. I drove there from Lake Te Anau, largest of the South Island lakes and sited on the fringe of Fiordland. The scenic and varied route enters the Eglinton Valley and then follows the Eglinton River for many kilometres; forest and giant beech trees (up to thirty metres high) flank the road. After passing Lake Lochie, it is not long before the white peak of Mount Christina (more than 2·5 kilometres) can be seen rising above the skyline, seeming to emerge from the centre of deep forest. Here the road descends the precipitous sides of a U-shaped glacial valley. This rugged grandeur continues for another 24 kilometres, as far as the entrance to Homer Tunnel where thousands of tons of avalanche ice and snow are scattered for kilometres over the valley floor, leaving only mountain scrub where thick forest once grew. Such is the power and destructive force of an avalanche. In a matter of seconds, it will hurl murderous masses of rock, ice and earth in one giant wave that can engulf entire towns and sweep away everything standing in its path.

I have experienced very small avalanches in the Swiss Alps, and standing here at the tunnel entrance my spine chilled as I realized the immensity of these particular slides. It was easy to imagine that first crash, like thunder; the cloud of snow dust beginning to career down the mountainside; the rumbling that grows louder, until it is almost deafening; the enormous boulders being hurled and bounced high into the sky, as if they were pebbles, before falling across the valley in a rain of death. Now the mountains were quiet, as they looked down upon the cars and tourist coaches; but, at any moment, with one tiny flick of their rocky fingers, they could halt these scuttling ants and re-establish the supremacy of nature.

Pages 78-79:
Another area of geysers and bubbling mud pots is at Whakarewarewa (better known as Whaka), an area less than 1.5 kilometres south of Rotorua. Occasionally, the Pohutu Geyser will throw scalding water more than twenty metres high. For those with little time to spare, Whaka is fascinating but in no way can rival the ultimate experience of Waimangu—*page 80*.

The tunnel, almost one kilometre long, was blasted through the sheer walls of the Homer Saddle. The road then cuts through the narrow Cleddau Canyon and across a mighty chasm while steeply descending for almost 900 metres to the head of Milford Sound. Clusters of derelict huts and ghost camps are reminders of the brave men who worked on this lonely project; yet, I expect few visitors stop to think about the effort, planning, frustration, danger, tragic accidents and conquest that went into making their passage swift and safe.

A MASTERPIECE OF CREATION

Milford Sound, a great canyon which knifes in from the sea, was created during an ice age. Forests and blue ice-cliffs rise sheer from the water to a height of several thousand kilometres, thereby providing one of the most dramatic scenes in New Zealand. The first men to see Milford were possibly Maui and his Polynesian followers who must have found it difficult to associate this icy land with their warm, palm-fringed Matavai Bay in Tahiti. Yet, this was but another location along one of their diverse trails across the Pacific. Certainly Fiordland was the limit of their travel in the newly discovered 'long white cloud', but further south, the Antarctic waited. Even now, I had not reached the end of their wide Pacific world; what amazing people they must have been!

For many years, access to the Sound was either by sea or overland, the latter way being along the famous fifty-three-kilometre Milford Track, often called 'WonderWalk of the World'.

This track is still passable and every year it attracts the more adventurous tourists who start from the track office at Te Anau Hotel, where packs and waterproof capes are available free of charge.

In many ways the track provides an experience not far removed from that of the explorers of eighty years ago who discovered this route to Milford Sound. There is still a mountain pass to be conquered (almost one kilometre high); there are still rivers to cross, even though the larger ones are now bridged; and there is still heavy rain which is just as prevalent in this part of Fiordland as it was a century ago.

The route itself (and even the siting of the huts) is virtually the same as when Quinton Mackinnon opened the track commercially in 1889. The huts are really 'lodges' and, with Dunlopillo mattresses, electricity, modern toilets and many other facilities, they give the present-day trampers somewhat different overnight accommodation from the pioneers. But apart from this concession to comfort, little has altered. Certainly the track is a good reason for abandoning the car and setting out on foot, especially when people are just beginning to worry that the internal combustion engine, coupled with easy chairs and television, might be responsible for starting the evolution of man's legs from means of transport to useless limbs! So, why not walk? For millions of years walking was mankind's only means of locomotion. And those who retrace the steps of the early pioneers will be rewarded with the towering rock walls of Clinton Canyon, the same mighty

PANIA
OF THE REEF
AN OLD MAORI LEGEND
TELLS HOW PANIA, LURED
BY THE SIREN VOICES OF
THE SEA PEOPLE, SWAM OUT
TO MEET THEM. WHEN SHE
ENDEAVOURED TO RETURN TO
HER LOVER, SHE WAS TRANS
-FORMED INTO THE REEF
WHICH NOW LIES BEYOND
THE NAPIER BREAKWATER.
TO PERPETUATE THE LEGEND
THE THIRTY THOUSAND CLUB
PRESENTED THIS STATUE TO
THE CITY OF NAPIER - 1954

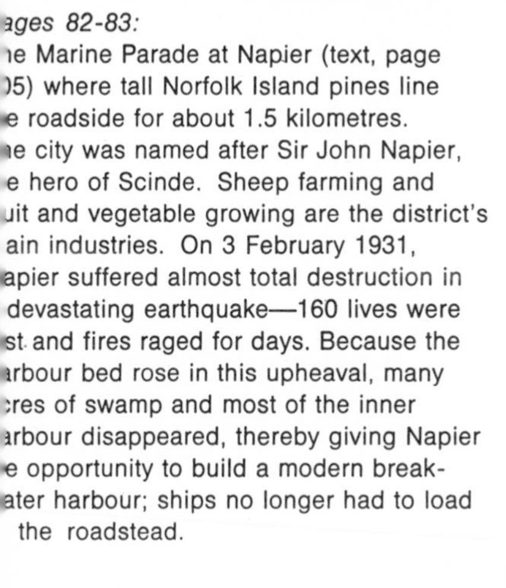

ages 82-83:
ıe Marine Parade at Napier (text, page
)5) where tall Norfolk Island pines line
e roadside for about 1.5 kilometres.
ıe city was named after Sir John Napier,
e hero of Scinde. Sheep farming and
uit and vegetable growing are the district's
ain industries. On 3 February 1931,
apier suffered almost total destruction in
devastating earthquake—160 lives were
st and fires raged for days. Because the
ırbour bed rose in this upheaval, many
:res of swamp and most of the inner
ırbour disappeared, thereby giving Napier
e opportunity to build a modern break-
ater harbour; ships no longer had to load
the roadstead.

At Napier's Marineland, dolphins give amazing performances. While these sleek-bodied fish are swift and gentle, it is known their brains are larger and, in some ways, more complex than man's. They are friendly, intelligent, warm-blooded mammals with a built-in grin; fun-loving animals who appear to enjoy crowds. If they did not enjoy such antics, scientists believe the strong-willed dolphins would react violently. But at Marineland they show no hostility—just wide toothy grins with the 'ring of confidence' that helps to maintain their name of deep-sea jesters. It is hard to believe these tolerant creatures are able to protect themselves against any shark foolish enough to attack.

Sutherland Falls hurtling down from an invisible lake, the same great valleys and majestic fiords.

People who walk gain a philosophical sustenance; they discover and rediscover themselves and the world in a thousand different ways. It was an American naturalist and philosopher who in 1870 wrote, 'Methinks that the moment my legs begin to move, my thoughts begin to flow.' In particular, the Milford Track, while remaining a challenge without demanding unsurpassed stamina and toughness, offers an 'aloneness' that provides a communication with nature desired by so many.

Once at Milford, visitors can see this inspiring waterway of the world from comfortable launches which ply back and forth across the icy waters, passing close to the many gigantic falls that spill from lofty mountainlocked lakes. Some of the landmarks, seen from these launches, include:

Bowen Falls: Dropping 159 metres from a hanging valley in the Darran Range. They are most spectacular an hour or two after rain.

Sinbad Gully: An example of a hanging valley; slopes steeply, between Mount Phillips and Mitre Peak, to the Llawrenny Peaks.

Mitre Peak: Rises 1668 metres from the sea; so named because it resembles a bishop's headdress.

Dale Point: On one side of the inner entrance to the Sound.

Anita Bay: Famed for 'tangiwai', the unique flecked greenstone which attracted the Maoris to Fiordland, and which can still be picked up on the beach.

Little Matter-horn: The valley above the Stirling Falls.

Stirling Falls: Between the Elephant and the Lion peaks.

Harrison Cove: At the mouth of the Brunhilde River which flows from the foot of the Pembroke Glacier; the only anchorage for ships.

Pembroke Peak and Glacier: Named after the Welsh county and town. The glacier is the remnant of a tributary to the vanished glacier which gouged out Milford Sound.

Sheerdown Range: Forms a sixteen-kilometre wall to the Cleddau Canyon which is followed by the road to Te Anau.

Arthur River: Followed by the last stage of the Milford Track to Sandfly Point, where trampers embark for the last part of their journey. It passes by Deepwater Basin, a former anchorage.

New Zealand
Electricity
Danger
Scalding hot water
Keep away

New Zealand
Electricity
Wairakei Geothermal
Power Station
Information Centre

Pages 86-88: ▷
At Wairakei, geothermal steam has been harnessed to produce electricity. (Text, pages 105 and 109.) There are conducted tours around this natural power plant as well as around many other attractions (thermal and scenic) within easy reach. Huka Falls, Geyser Valley, Aratiatia Rapids and Karapiti Blowhole are but four of the sights for which Wairakei is a centre.

Profile-Four Cities

WELLINGTON, the capital of New Zealand, was named after the first Duke of Wellington. The city's motto, *Suprema a Situ* (Supreme by Situation), reflects the pride of being a huge amphitheatre surrounded by the hills of Port Nicholson. To fully appreciate the site, drive to the lookout, at the top of Mount Victoria (197 metres), from where there is a panorama of Hutt Valley, the city and its harbour with 67 kilometres of foreshore. A marine drive passes through numerous attractive bays from where the snow-covered mountains of South Island can be seen on clear days.

A commercial and political centre, Wellington houses the head offices of national and international organizations as well as government departments. (The old Government Building of 1876, built from about 300 kilometres of New Zealand timber, is believed to be the world's biggest wooden structure.) The ever-increasing number of highrise office blocks is visual proof of the vigorous commercial and economic growth. Indeed, because of this swift expansion, Wellington has been said to be 'a city marching up the hills'; and it is hard to believe that little more than a century ago the first shipload of organized settlers arrived in the small barque *Tory*.

Modern buildings include the National War Memorial Carillon of forty-nine bells, the National Art Gallery, and the Dominion Museum with its unrivalled collection of Maori artefacts.

There are even a few 'nightclubs', which in New Zealand are mostly non-existent. I visited the best one of them; a handful of attractive girls, plus a few dozen singularly unattractive girls, performed partial and full striptease on an unadorned stage to the accompaniment of recorded music. At the time, the club had not been granted a licence to sell liquor, so I sat drinking Coca-Cola which did little to help overcome the bleak atmosphere. Nevertheless, two or three dancers had reasonable expertise; and a dark-skinned, large-bosomed girl, who had covered her body in olive oil, appeared to delight the spectators (mainly Japanese) with a sensual, writhing, shaking and quivering routine that sprayed droplets of oil across the stage as her 'acrobatics' reached a climax. If you are desperate for entertainment, or have lived in a desert for years, this kind of evening may be great; but I doubt if it would thrill very many overseas visitors.

However, Wellington does offer limitless attractions *by day*: from

A typical placid old-world scene to be
found within a few kilometres of the capital
or of any of the biggest cities.

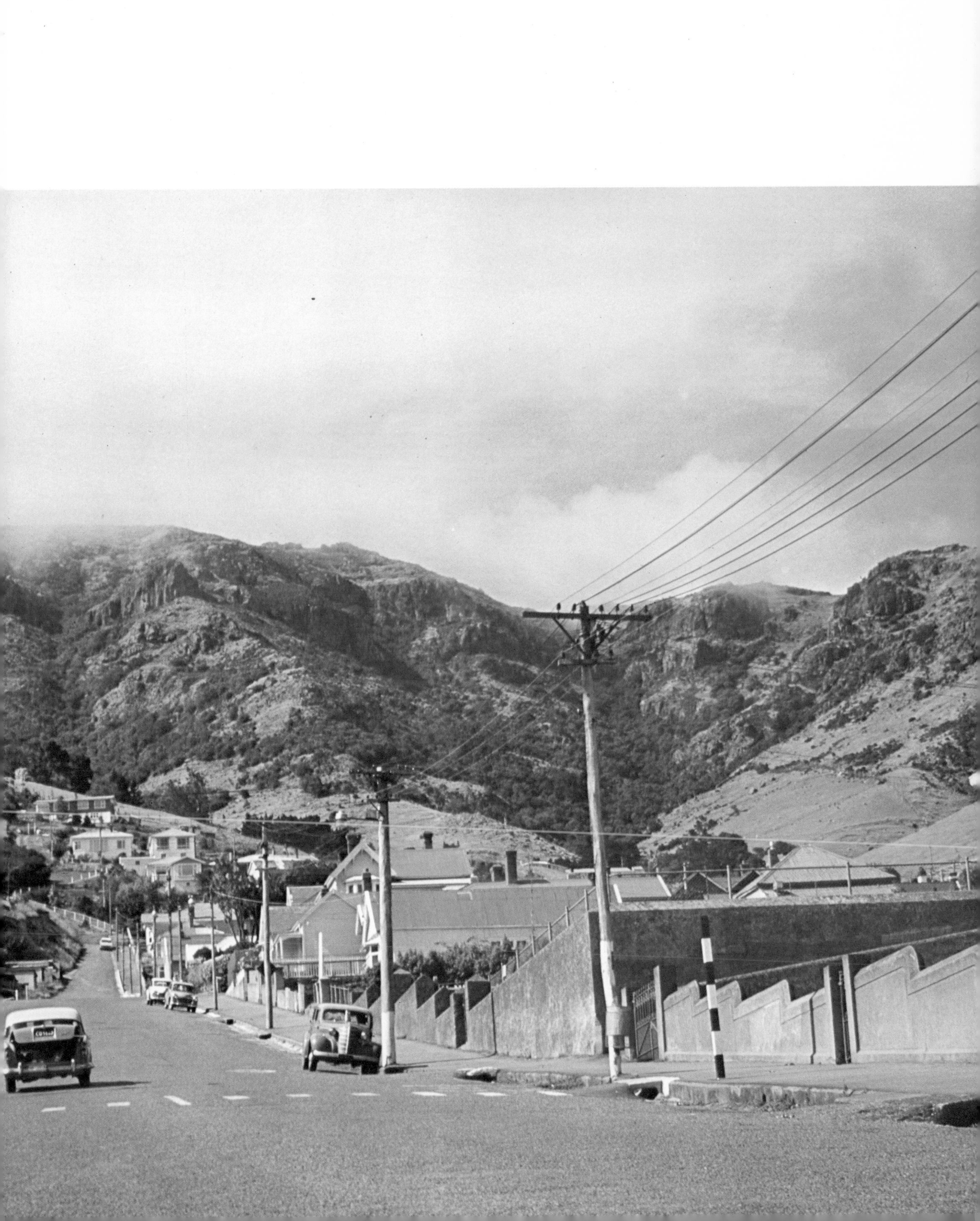

Page 94: ▷
Everywhere in New Zealand there are attractive girls. This young lady was working for the government, in tourism.

excellent shopping to almost 800 hectares of reserve land, which includes fine botanical gardens, Otari Native Flora Reserve, and the 260-hectare Williams Park consisting largely of native bush, which is a home for New Zealand birds in their natural habitat.

CHRISTCHURCH, the next largest city to Auckland, was founded in the nineteenth century, by English gentlemen, on a site that was once described as 'the most dismal part of the Canterbury Plains comprising miles of mud, mire and marsh'. But equally, in 1842, it was said of Hong Kong, 'Here is an island lacking in everything except rocks, salt, water and pirates; it seems obvious never to be a mart of trade.' In less than one hundred years after this statement was made, Hong Kong was a booming commercial centre and seaport. Christchurch, after a similarly poor start to life, likewise blossomed quickly into prosperity and a quiet beauty in which enthusiastic home-owners compete for officially designated 'diplomas' that recognize the best garden and most pleasing street as a whole.

Indeed, the gardens with their trim green lawns, the willows on the banks of the Avon River (legend says they came from Napoleon's grave on St Helena), the famed Canterbury Cathedral with bells that are duplicates of the upper 10 in London's St Paul's Cathedral, and even bright red buses, all helped Christchurch to become known as 'the most English city out of England'. Little has really changed; and improved but contemporary building development has produced an attractive blend of the old and the new; it is still very much an English garden-city where the botanic reserve, which imported many species from England's Kew Gardens, is classed as being among the world's top ten.

South of the city are the Port Hills, along which extend thirty-nine kilometres of summit road overlooking the Canterbury Plains and Southern Alps.

It is not a swinging city, but is dignified, graceful and beautiful with an atmosphere of peace rather than pace. In this busy world Christchurch brings a welcome change that 'grows' on a visitor.

DUNEDIN, the port and capital of Otago, while retaining much of its original Scottish character, also has the imprint of the periodic invasions that give its history of early settlement more interest than any other New Zealand city. First came the Maoris, then the whalers. Later, shiploads of Scottish Free Church immigrants landed over a long period. The discovery of gold in 1861 brought a cosmopolitan mixture of diggers from Australia, North America, Britain and China, swelling the population of Otago Province by about 65 000. Shanty towns were everywhere. Epidemics raged and the death rate was high, but in four years Otago exported $14 million worth of gold. Finally, there arrived from all countries an abundance of business and commercial men who brought a diversity of new culture and economic techniques.

But even while prosperity was at its height, the canny Scots realized the boom could not last forever and they began to establish more permanent

ages 96 to 98:
he barren, rocky, ice landscapes of a
acier valley.

industries like fruit growing, cattle raising, and farming. Their foresight was wise because the gold supplies inevitably dwindled and economic growth began to decline.

Now, Dunedin is only the fifth largest city; but it is once again beginning a new life, this time as a manufacturing centre, a busy port, and the gateway to the scenic attractions of Central Otago. For the visitor, there are fine shops and a host of beautiful churches, schools, and gardens. It is also very much a city of the arts, and a list of the past presidents of the Dunedin Society reads like a 'Who's Who of New Zealand's Art World'.

Well worth a visit is Lanarch Castle, the private home of Mr and Mrs Barry Barker, who are now restoring some of the building's former graciousness. The castle was built in 1871 by the Hon. W. J. M. Lanarch who came from Australia to manage the first bank in Otago. Two hundred workmen took three years to complete the 'shell' and a further twelve years were spent on embellishing the interior. The total cost was £125 000 which, in current New Zealand value, is equal to about $3 million. Lanarch had married a French heiress, which explains this sumptuous residence in a struggling colonial town barely twenty years old.

While first impressions of Dunedin may be disappointing, those who are not just 'passing through' will be pleasantly surprised.

AUCKLAND, built on a narrow isthmus between two beautiful harbours, is the biggest city in New Zealand.

Thousands of years ago a great volcanic upheaval left scores of craters and cones which now form the charming natural basins and hillsides of Auckland. Innumerable battles were fought over the possession of this prized isthmus, where the peaks still show terraced trench systems which once surrounded Maori forts, but which now form parks and gardens. These green areas are oases in a rapidly expanding city which has almost 750 000 people, nearly one-third of the combined population of North and South Island. Nevertheless, it is gracious and well planned. From the summit of Mount Eden, an extinct volcano, there is a full-circle panorama: kilometres of coastline scalloped by fine beaches; a sprinkling of offshore islands (Waiheke and Pakatoa are reached by hydrofoil), some less than 800 years old; dozens of reserve areas merging with the green of twenty-four golf courses; verdant hillsides where sheep graze within 5 kilometres of Queen Street, the main shopping centre; a fine racecourse; thermal springs; and twin harbours. (On Anniversary Day, the nearest Monday to 29 January, the largest one-day regatta in the world is held for yachts of all classes, starting from Waitemata Harbour—*Sea of Sparkling Waters*—so aptly named by the Maoris.) Ferry trips across the harbour are always worthwhile.

Motorways spread in all directions while the busy city and residential North Shore are connected by a bridge with eight traffic lanes.

Auckland is definitely the liveliest city in New Zealand. Every year it becomes more robustious, asserting a personal vigour that indicates its urgent desire to become a vital city of the South-West Pacific; a destiny that would seem to be inevitable over the coming years.

Pages 100-103: ▷
Even for a pilot, to land on the Tasman Glacier is an aerial-scenic experience never to be forgotten. And the Tasman is one of the largest glaciers in the world outside the Himalayas and Polar regions. These pictures, by courtesy of Mount Cook Airlines, show a Cessna 'turning final' for its landing approach on the glacier. The pilot must exercise great skill and judgment, but to these veterans of the air, it is no more difficult than landing on miles of paved runway! (Text, pages 47 to 59.)

Left:
Leaving the Cessna, I noisily crunched my way across this solitude of ice.
Right:
Air speed, manifold pressure, revolutions, oil/engine temperatures, fuel mixture and 'attitude'; a dozen instruments provide all this information which is so vital when flying in mountainous terrain.

Pages 104-108: ▷
Somewhere in New Zealand, at any time of the year, visitors can nearly always find a place to ski. And when there is no snow, then chairlifts are used merely to admire the view.

Just Wandering–Wellington to Rotorua

Napier is a seaside resort one hour by air from Wellington. Sheltered by the Ruahine and Kaweka Ranges, the climate is particularly warm and pleasant. According to a travel brochure, an Australian journalist termed Napier 'New Zealand's Switched-on City' and, instead of staying two days, he remained for ten because there was so much to see and do. Since that comment, Napier must have blown its fuse! Apart from a marine drive where the gardens are attractive, the resort seems to offer little except some amazing dolphins which perform at Marineland. *I* was scheduled to stay for three days and left after two, deciding to make for Wairakei by road. The drive is worthwhile, and the journey covers a diversity of scenery that is so typical of this country: coastline, mountains, bushland, forests, plains, turbulent rivers, waterfalls, and Taupo, the biggest lake in New Zealand and famous for outsized rainbow trout.

NATURE'S POWER HOUSE

Wairakei is characterized by perpetually rising clouds of steam and a subdued roar. Both emanate from man's efforts to harness natural underground steam to generate electricity.

The first experiments to harness geothermal steam took place in Italy before the turn of the century, and the first electricity was produced at Lardarello, Italy, in 1913.

The world's second geothermal power station was built at Wairakei, which lies on an active volcanic zone extending north-east from Mount Ruapehu in the centre of North Island, through Taupo and Rotorua, to White Island in the Bay of Plenty. The powerhouse is sited beside the Waikato River, and uses steam from more than sixty bores drilled in the nearby Waiora Valley to depths approaching 1·25 kilometres.

The Wairakei scheme is based on the tapping of a vast underground hot-water system, believed to result from contact between subterranean water supplies and very hot, perhaps even molten, rock. The rock strata at Wairakei includes a porous mass below a layer of dense sandstone. At 600 metres there is a massive strata of volcanic flow rock called ignimbrite where high-temperature water seeps through cracks up into the porous layer. Steam is obtained by drilling a bore which, in releasing the pressure on this

very hot water, causes it to boil. By drilling anywhere in the porous strata, steam can be obtained at shallow depths; but only by drilling deep and close to one of the near-vertical cracks in the lower strata can high pressure steam be obtained.

In 1971, sixty-one bores were supplying steam to the station—twenty-nine at high pressure and thirty-two at intermediate pressure. Pipelines take the steam to the Wairakei Geothermal-Steam Station which feeds into the North Island grid system at 220 000 volts.

Five kilometres away it is possible to visit the Karapiti Blowhole, a 'power' jet where steam, according to the Maoris, has been erupting at tremendous pressure for at least 500 years. Just 12 years ago, there was a further increase in activity when new craters and fumaroles appeared; these were followed by two great mud craters which give the impression of a lunar landscape.

THERMAL SAFARI

Rotorua is the centre of New Zealand's thermal region where geysers, hot springs, boiling mud pools and every other kind of volcanic activity hiss roar, spout, pop, or bubble at the visitor; occasionally, even flowerbeds alongside the road will puff out a few 'smoke rings'! Water-heaters are definitely not in demand because residents get all the domestic hot water they require simply by putting down a shallow bore in their garden. And the air—especially after rain—has a distinctive but not unpleasant smell that I can best describe as a sulphury ozone, or something like burnt gunpowder after a firework display.

However, the most impressive thermal activities are all concentrated in the Waimangu Valley, just 25 kilometres from Rotorua. This valley was created on 10 June 1886 by an eruption of Mount Tarawera; it blew away the entire south-western face of the mountain, opened a 16-kilometre rift along the entire range, buried the village of Te Wairoa and left a steaming crater with sides 244 metres high. Never, in my extensive travels throughout the world, have I seen any other thermal areas that are so excitingly impressive or so weirdly fascinating; the valley is a phenomenon that displaces time and can transport an active mind way back to 'the age of creation'.

A safe pathway winds for about 6·5 kilometres through Waimangu. At first it falls steeply, leading past Emerald Pool, the most southerly crater formed by Tarawera's eruption and now filled with jade green water. Here is absolute silence. Nothing stirs on the landscape—not a tree, not a blade of grass. Next are Echo Crater and Waimangu Cauldron where, in 1917, an unexpected volcanic explosion destroyed the Government Accommodation House. The Cauldron, occupying four hectares, is full of boiling water which has a flow outlet exceeding five kilolitres a minute. Rising out of Waimangu, the Cathedral Rocks thrust skywards. These craggy pinnacles often disappear entirely in dense clouds of billowing steam. The path carries on past boiling springs and the site of a geyser, once the world's largest with water being hurled to an altitude of 457 metres; a white cross marks the spot where a guide and three visitors died during the first eruption

Left/right:
Maori, Pakeha, woodcarver, weaver, dancer —everywhere the tourist finds interesting people, different faces, men and women in unusual occupations.

Valleys, mountains, lakes—reflections and shadows; an ever-changing pattern of light.

in 1903. Still descending, one arrives at Ruaumoko's Throat, a deep, almost circular crater, full of pulsating milky-blue water of unknown depth. Shrouded in steam it has an incredible rate of flow, and occasionally it recedes by 15 metres to uncover crater walls of shining white silica. This is a highlight of the Waimangu trail which finally ends on the lovely shores of Lake Rotomahana.

Apart from Waimangu Valley, Rotorua offers the tourist a tremendously wide range of attractions.

Those who wish to bathe in Rotorua's thermal waters can visit *Polynesian Pools* where natural mineral springs have been used for almost a century. This beautifully appointed complex has a big, separate pool for children and adults, and another one for adults only. Fourteen luxurious private pools —with carpeted and heated dressing rooms—are all fed, by the famous Rachel Spring, with an alkaline, sulphuretted water which is an emollient to the skin and a sedative in reaction. A rumour among locals says it also has aphrodisiac qualities; the more sceptical say it is only the normal 'body chemistry' triggered off when a couple bathe nude in a hot, bubbling, spring bath almost large enough for swimming. But I can vouch for the refreshing, sedative reaction and I will make a point of visiting Rotorua again. As for the sceptics—even though I bathed alone, it is sufficient to say that they may be very wrong! For those who suffer any specific nervous tension or rheumatic disorder, stronger waters are available in the Priest and Radium Springs which bubble out of pumice. (The Priest has 'free acid' water, due to the presence of sulphuric acid; it is stimulating and tonic in reaction. The Radium is also 'acid', but is especially effective for muscular troubles.)

Polynesian Pools are owned and run by a Mr W. E. Lobb who acquired the spa only recently. His remodelling of the complex (in decor and policy) has completely transformed it from the years when it was apparently run in a drab, institutional manner for elderly people and when men and women were always segregated, both in the big and the private baths. Now, the *Pools* are attracting young folk in ever-increasing numbers, and I predict a visit here will become the 'in' thing.

In addition to thermal attractions, Rotorua is also a focal point of New Zealand's Maori cult. Maoris take pride in keeping alive their ancient heritage and they present regular performances of their old chants, dances, and rhythm games. The Maori settlement of Whakarewarewa has a model fortified village, maintained in the traditional style, and houses the Maori Arts and Crafts Centre where visitors can watch skilled woodcarvers at work. Those who wish to know the Maori people better receive many opportunities: the young Maori boy attending the motel bar, the local chemist, a waitress, the postman, even a woman taxi driver; these were just a few of the friends I made. 'Accept us as you find us' is their attitude. I found them to be warm-hearted people who, exactly like the early Polynesians, still welcome the stranger in to their homes, where they live with parents, brothers, sisters, relations and friends in 'open' communal houses of ever-changing occupants. When I was invited into their living rooms, no questions were asked. They

Suburbia. Every house a different design. No two streets the same. But all colourful and modern. This aspect alone makes New Zealand cities unique. (See Christchurch; text, page 95.)

ge 120: ▷
e Canterbury Pilgrims made their
storic trek over the steep Port Hills to
rtile plains such as these wild acres,
hich carry more than one million sheep.

arvings which typify the age-old skill of
aori art.

accepted me immediately, and life carried on normally—talking, eating, singing, drinking, loving, sleeping, watching television. It was impossible to feel a stranger in this environment.

So, where I had shortened my stay in Napier, I kept adding days at Rotorua. Even then, I spent too little time at places like Fairy Springs with its crystal clear water, Round Lake, Paradise Valley, and Mokoia Island (special moonlight cruises with a barbecue).

THE PERFECT WAY

From Rotorua I was at the controls of a twin-engine Baron, flying at 10 000 feet in blue sky above a light, cloud strata. There was little to do except an occasional minor adjustment of power, a check of the ADF (Automatic Direction Finder), and a quick scan of engine instruments: oil, manifold and fuel pressures; cylinder-head and oil temperatures; suction gauges; and fuel flow. Everything was operating normally, with needles centred well off the red and yellow radials. It was not long before I was 'letting down' to the Auckland approach. I reduced power. The altimeter began to unwind, and, in seconds, the cloud strata had passed. Below me lay that green New Zealand world which was once described as 'like a big park when seen from the air'. At 140 knots, I lowered the wheels; green lights shone reassuringly. Now, mixture controls full rich, propellors in low pitch, cowlings closed, main tanks selected, fuel boost pumps at low. At 120 knots, I depressed the flap lever to its *full down 28°* position; this time a red light glowed. The descent angle steepened as I maintained a speed of about 101 knots on my final shallow turn. Just a little too fast, but I still believed in the old pilots' adage, 'an extra five knots for the wife and another five for the kids'. Once on the straight approach, I quickly 'dumped' extra speed (by raising the nose slightly) to come-in normally at about 90 knots, holding-off, and making contact gently.

It was a good landing and a perfect way to end my journey through a country which, perhaps more than any other developing nation, owes its progress to the aeroplane. As late as the 1940s much of South Island was inaccessible except by foot. Even today, a trip that takes twenty minutes by air can mean a difficult, twisting, nine-hour, car journey over mountain roads. Likewise, the process of aerial top-dressing (devised by New Zealanders) has turned once barren land into productive pastures. And, with modern jets, New Zealand is no longer isolated from the world: three hours from Australia, one day from Japan, three days from Britain, and two days from North and South America.

As the most varied and interesting 'travel package' in the Pacific area, New Zealand can be called a monument to man's cooperation with nature: an evolution from a violent cataclysmic birth to a green holiday wonderland, almost completely unspoiled by technological progress.

To paraphrase an advertising slogan: 'Go to New Zealand. Now!'

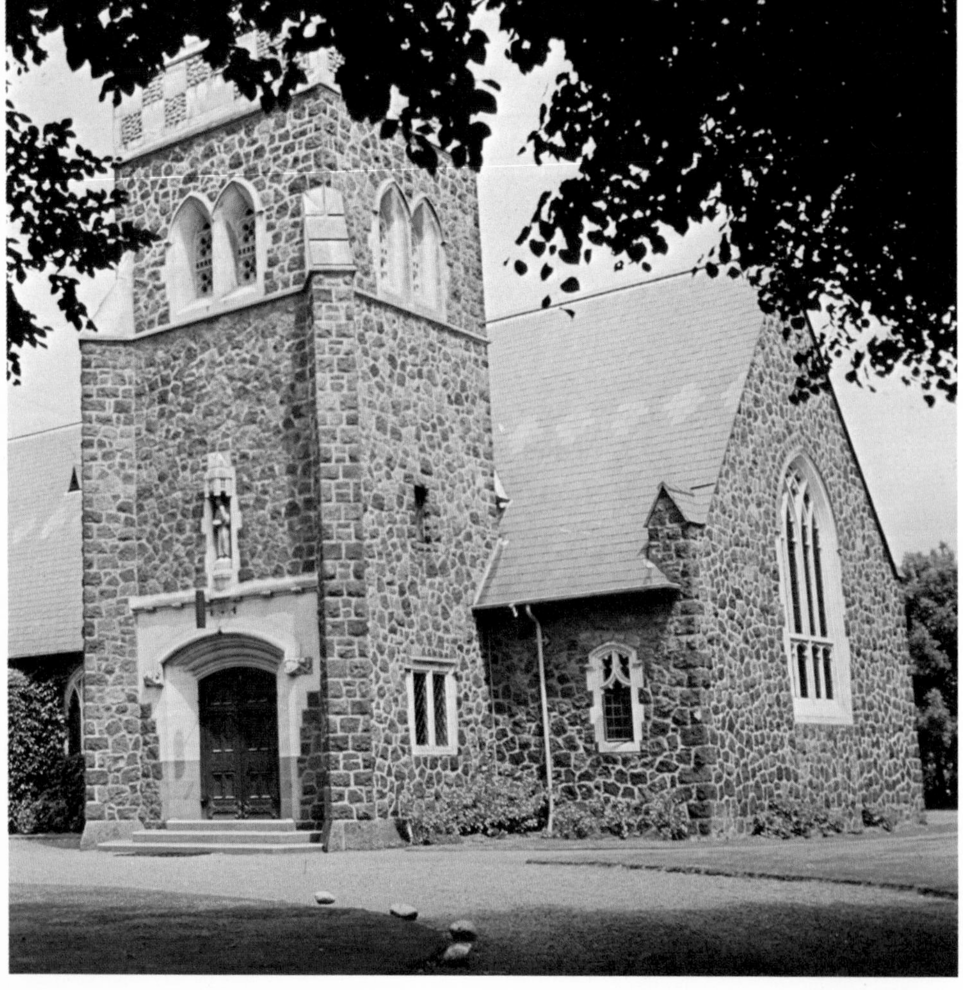

The old and the new are all blended with great skill and dignity – churches, universities (*bottom left/top left* – Christchurch), houses, offices, post offices, banks.
Pages 124-125: ▷
Auckland Harbour Bridge by night, a glittering 'monument' that cost $26 million.

WHAKAREWAREWA
POST OFFICE

Notes on Photographic Equipment

For those interested in the technical aspects of photography, the following equipment was used.

Equipment:

(a) The Hasselblad 500/CM single-lens 6 x 6 cm square reflex camera with a 2.8/80 mm Carl Zeiss Planar as standard, plus the Zeiss 4/50 mm Distagon, the Zeiss 4/150 mm Sonnar and the Zeiss 8/500 mm Tele-Tessar. After having worked for many years with a Rolleiflex, I have recently converted to Hasselblad. It is fantastic equipment, which has specifications of an advanced 35 mm camera (reflex viewfinding, interchangeable lenses, fast return mirror) plus the additional features of interchangeable magazines accepting normal "120" size roll film, a fine-focusing magnifier and a rapid-winding crank. Furthermore, the Hasselblad lenses have a built-in Synchro-Compur shutter with automatic diaphragm, an "exposure-value" scale (EVS), automatic depth-of-field indicator, and fully synchronized M, X and V settings; lenses are attached by a quick-action bayonet fitting. The depth-of-field indicator is so functional that it can be used for actual focus settings (extremely accurate) as well as for determining hyperfocal distances. Viewfinding is always at full aperture but, by depressing a small catch, the pre-set (or "working") aperture is immediately selected so that a *visual* check can be made for depth-of-field effects; exposure values are quickly disengaged to give full control over aperture and speed combinations. All these lens features enable me to focus and to control focus depth to within finer limits than ever previously. Interchangeable magazines mean no wasted time for loading and no wasted film—either when changing from monochrome to colour or when, for a certain subject, it is desirable to have a full twelve exposures available. There is even a speeded-up shutter release which opens the auxiliary (magazine) shutter in advance of pressing the release button and thereby reduces actual exposure times to a minimum. Finally, an unbelievable range of accessories makes the Hasselblad capable of tackling any kind of photography, from underwater to macro-work, in any conditions.

(b) I also used a 6 x 6 cm Rolleiflex Model 2.8/80 mm and a 35 mm Canon QLFT, the latter with lenses of 1.4/50 mm, 2.5/35 mm and 2.5/135 mm. Rolleiflex cameras have given me years of faithful service in tough climates all over the world. If the Hasselblad is just as rugged—and it certainly appears to be—then, as soon as my "familiarization" period is complete, the Hasselblad will make both the Rollei and Canon equipment an unnecessary burden for my particular needs. All future books can be photographed exclusively with this 500C/M which I consider a magnificent piece of optical technology.

Exposure Meter:

A Weston Master V with invercone for incident light readings; particularly useful for colour work.

Filters:

A standard range of colour correction filters used only in light conditions of extremely high or low colour temperature; an ultraviolet filter; and a "pola" screen for selective control over (1) reflections from non-metallic objects and (2) light from a clear blue sky when at right-angles to the direction of the sun; a "pola" screen is the only means of darkening a blue sky without distorting the colour reproduction of other objects.

Film:

All photographs were made on Kodak Ektachrome-X, daylight type, and exposed for the recommended ASA rating of 64. Film was processed by Spectrum Laboratories, Queensland, Australia.

Occasionally, a National Auto Pana computing electronic flash unit was used for "fill-in" only; no other additional light sources of any kind were employed.

Further details about New Zealand
can be obtained either from

New Zealand Government Tourist Bureaux

or from

Overseas Travel Information Service.
Box 284, Toowong, Queensland 4066,
Australia.

▽